MW01235119

STANDARD BOOK OF

DIOR

timeless elegance

Chloé Kamali-Worth

STANDARD BOOK OF

DIOR

1946

CHLOE KAMALI-WORTH

Christian Dior was a highly influential French fashion designer, born on January 21, 1905 in Granville, Normandy, France. He is best known for having founded one of the largest fashion houses in the world, also called "Dior", in 1946.

Dior's impact on fashion was monumental, particularly through the creation of the "New Look" which debuted in 1947. This style was in stark contrast to the fabric-saving styles of the World War II era.

The "New Look" featured rounded shoulders, a cinched waist and a full A-shaped skirt. This design celebrated opulence and femininity, having a significant impact on women's fashion and re-establishing Paris as the center of the fashion world after the war.

The codes of DIOR luxury

Sophisticated Aesthetics: Dior is known for its elegant and timeless designs. The Dior aesthetic often combines classic femininity with subtle modernity.

Craftsmanship and quality: An essential element of Dior luxury is meticulous attention to detail and high-quality craftsmanship. Whether it is haute couture, ready-to-wear, accessories or perfumes, each product is the result of exceptional know-how.

Innovation: While Dior respects its traditions, the brand is also known for its innovative approach to fashion and design, incorporating new technologies and ideas while remaining true to its aesthetic heritage.

Legacy and History: Christian Dior's legacy and his revolutionary impact on fashion with the "New Look" continues to influence the collections. This historical richness is a crucial aspect of Dior luxury.

The exclusive customer experience: Dior offers its customers a premium experience, whether in stores, at fashion shows or in online interactions. The emphasis is on customization and exceptional customer service.

Symbolism and iconography: elements such as the cannage motif, the Dior rose (in homage to Christian Dior's favorite flower) and emblematic colors such as Dior gray and powder pink, are distinctive aesthetic codes of the brand.

Ambassadors and collaborations: Brand ambassadors, often celebrities and influential figures, as well as collaborations with renowned artists and designers, contribute to Dior's prestige and luxury image.

01

Dior, founded by Christian Dior in 1946, is famous for its revolutionary **"New Look"** style, which redefined women's fashion after World War II with its voluptuous and elegant silhouettes.

02

Miss Dior, the first perfume launched by the Dior fashion house **in 1947**, embodies the very essence of elegance and femininity dear to Christian Dior. Conceived as a floral bouquet of sophistication and sophistication, this iconic fragrance continues to seduce women around the world with its captivating notes of rose, jasmine and patchouli, a testament to Dior's timeless legacy.

03

Over the decades, **under the leadership of designers such as Yves Saint Laurent and John Galliano,** Dior has maintained its reputation as a leader in luxury, known for its haute couture collections, iconic perfumes such as **"Miss Dior"** and **"J'adore "**, and its profound influence on the fashion industry and beyond.

From Haute Couture to Iconic Perfumes

Since its founding in 1946 by Christian Dior, the Dior fashion house has shaped the fashion industry with a distinctive blend of innovation and tradition. Over the decades, the brand has been led by visionary designers such as Yves Saint Laurent and John Galliano, who each brought their own unique touch while preserving the essence of the brand.

Under their leadership, Dior has strengthened its leading position in the world of luxury, producing haute couture collections that combine exquisite craftsmanship with avant-garde design.

These collections not only consolidated Dior's reputation as a symbol of elegance and sophistication, but also introduced revolutionary trends that redefined fashion several times.

In addition to its impact on high fashion, Dior has also left an indelible mark on the world of perfumes. Olfactory creations such as **"Miss Dior" and "J'adore" have become iconic icons,** each telling a unique story through their aromas. "Miss Dior", the first perfume launched by the house, embodies the spirit of femininity and elegance, reflecting the fundamental principles of Christian Dior himself.

With "J'adore", Dior has captured the essence of modern luxury, offering a fragrance that harmoniously blends floral and fruity notes. These iconic fragrances have strengthened Dior's status as a brand synonymous with sophistication, attracting a global and diverse clientele.

Dior's influence extends far beyond its tangible contributions to fashion and perfume; permeates popular culture and the fashion industry as a whole.

The brand has been a pioneer in developing fashion's visual identity through innovative advertising campaigns and collaborations with artists and celebrities. Shaping the aesthetic of elegance and luxury, Dior has inspired generations of designers and has continued to play a leading role in setting global fashion trends.

Dior's legacy, enriched by the contributions of its successive artistic directors, continues to thrive, a testament to its lasting impact on fashion and beyond.

04

In 1947, Christian Dior shook the fashion world with the launch of his first collection, dubbed the **"New Look,"** which introduced a radically new female silhouette characterized by cinched waists and voluminous skirts. This stylistic revolution not only redefined the standards of post-war feminine elegance, but also reaffirmed Paris as the undisputed capital of haute couture.

The dawn of a revolution: behind Dior's "New Look".

In 1947, in the heart of a Paris still marked by the consequences of the war, a stylistic revolution was about to see the light, a revolution that would redefine women's fashion and reaffirm Paris' role as the world capital of high fashion. sewing. This revolution had a name: the "New Look", a bold and visionary collection by Christian Dior. But behind this emblematic collection lies an anecdote that underlines the audacity and determination of its creator.

Christian Dior, then a young couturier, had a vision: to give women back their femininity and elegance, erased by years of conflict and austerity. She dreamed of floral silhouettes, narrow waists and voluminous skirts: in stark contrast to the pragmatic and thrifty style dictated by the circumstances of the time. When his first collection was ready to be presented, skepticism reigned, both among financiers and in the fashion industry itself. The luxurious fabrics and generous quantities used in his designs seemed almost provocative in a world still licking its wounds.

On the day of the presentation, February 12, 1947, the salon of the Dior house, located at 30 Avenue Montaigne, was packed. When the first models paraded, revealing new lines and opulence of fabrics, the public was speechless.

Carmel Snow, editor-in-chief of Harper's Bazaar magazine, exclaimed: **"My dear Christian, this is a completely new look!"** This spontaneous comment will not only christen the collection, but will also mark the beginning of a new era in fashion.

Dior's "New Look" was not just a fashion collection, it was a symbol of renewal and optimism, a breath of fresh air that allowed women to dream and aspire to beauty and elegance in a world under reconstruction.

This collection not only consolidated Christian Dior's reputation as one of the greatest couturiers of his time, but also revolutionized the way fashion was perceived and experienced.

05

Today, the "New Look" remains a testament to Dior's genius, reminding everyone that fashion is not just an art of adorning the body, but also a powerful expression of the spirit of the times. Behind every seam, every fold, there was the desire to restore hope and celebrate femininity in all its splendor. This is how Christian Dior entered history, not only as a couturier, but as a true visionary.

06

In the 1950s, the House of Dior introduced its iconic logo, adorned with the intertwined letters "CD", representing the initials of its founder, Christian Dior. This distinctive symbol soon became a guarantee of elegance and luxury, embodying the very essence of the brand throughout the world.

Renaissance and vision: the legacy of Christian Dior

A new era of fashion In the aftermath of the Second World War, a wind of change was blowing through Paris, **ready to embrace the revolutionary vision of a passionate pattern maker named Christian Dior.** On 12 February 1947, in the sumptuous setting of the salons at 30 Avenue Montaigne, Dior presented its first collection, marking the birth of the iconic Bar jacket. With creations symbolizing renewal and hope, Dior responded to the desire for beauty of a France marked by years of conflict.

The "New Look", so **named by Carmel Snow, editor-in-chief of Harper's Bazaar**, offered women a new silhouette, highlighting a forgotten femininity and elegance, characterized by voluminous skirts, narrow waists and highlighted chests.

The scent of seduction
For Christian Dior, the dress reaches its fullness only if accompanied by a perfume that sublimates its essence. Thus was born Miss Dior in 1947, a now timeless fragrance, which embodies the spirit of the Dior maison.

This olfactory creation, like the silhouettes of the collection, was a hymn to femininity and seduction, once again demonstrating Dior's holistic approach to fashion.

Expansion and leadership
Under the leadership of Christian Dior, the brand experienced meteoric expansion, establishing itself in fifteen countries in just ten years.

England and the United States were the first to embrace Dior's vision, thanks to a marketing strategy that was as ingenious as it was innovative. When Dior died in 1957, Yves Saint Laurent and then Marc Bohan took the reins, perpetuating the house's spirit of innovation and excellence.

The acquisition by the LVMH group in the early 1990s, followed by the arrival of John Galliano in 1996, brought a new creative dynamic, pushing Dior's turnover to unprecedented levels.

An unalterable heritage
Despite changes in direction and stylistic developments, the core values of refinement, elegance and excellence established by Christian Dior have survived.

Dior creations, always designed with passion and innovation, continue to fascinate the world of fashion, testifying to the brand's unwavering commitment to aesthetics and the realization of dreams.

Like that of the Bar jacket, immortalized in an iconic photo in which Dior employees meticulously adapt the model on the famous model Victoire, or the timid beginnings of Yves Saint Laurent, projected at the head of the Dior creation at just 21 years old, remind us that behind every Dior piece there is a story, a dream and an incessant search for beauty.

**Behind the scenes of the making of Dior's
Bar Mizza jacket**

Renaissance and vision: the legacy of Christian Dior

A new chapter on fashion

In the aftermath of the Second World War, the house of Dior, under the aegis of its visionary founder Christian Dior, opened a new chapter in the history of fashion. On 12 February 1947, at 30 Avenue Montaigne, an event would forever mark the world of high fashion: the presentation of Dior's first collection and, with it, the emblematic Bar Mizza jacket. This garment quickly became the symbol of the "New Look", an aesthetic revolution that supported an accentuated femininity, characterized by a marked waist, accentuated hips and unparalleled elegance.

The story goes that Christian Dior, passionate about architecture and shapes, spent hours perfecting the design of this jacket to achieve perfection.

The making of an icon

The Bar Mizza jacket is the result of exceptional know-how, an alchemy between tradition and innovation.

Every detail, from the choice of fabric to the final cut, is taken care of with meticulous attention. A famous anecdote has it that Dior, dissatisfied with the first prototypes, decided to reconstruct the jacket around a mannequin, pinching and adjusting the fabric until the silhouette exactly matched his vision.

This stubbornness gave birth to a jacket that not only redefined the female silhouette, but also embodied post-war renewal and optimism.

The symbol of an era

The Bar Mizza jacket wasn't just a fashion item; it was the symbol of a new era, it reflected the desire for beauty, happiness and elegance after the dark years of the war. He embodied hope and renewal and his success was immediate. Women all over the world aspired to adopt this "New Look", synonymous with refinement. The impact of this collection was such that the Bar jacket became a must-have in the women's wardrobe, a strong piece that reflects the genius and audacity of Christian Dior.

08

A legacy perpetuated
Today, the Bar Mizza jacket remains a pillar of
the identity of the house of Dior, a living
testimony to continuous innovation and
respect for traditions.

09

The artistic directors who succeeded Christian Dior have each interpreted this iconic piece in their own way, while remaining faithful to the original spirit of elegance and perfection. **The Bar Mizza jacket** embodies the essence of Dior: a fusion of art and fashion, an unconditional love for beauty and an incessant desire to reinvent elegance.

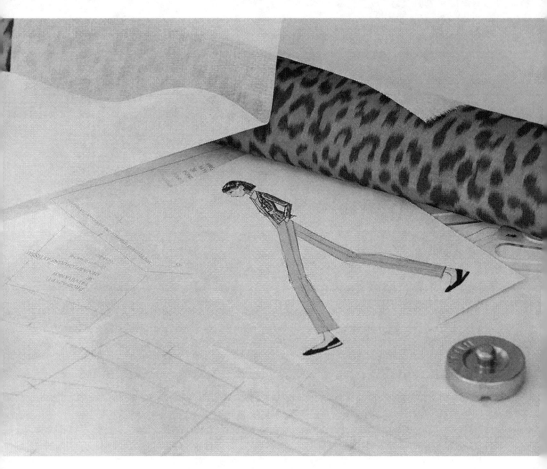

10

Through the Bar Mizza jacket, Dior continues to weave its story, uniting past, present and future in a perpetual celebration of fashion.

11

"J'adore" has become one of the best-selling fragrances in the world since its launch **in 1999**, embodying the very essence of femininity and luxury through its sophisticated floral notes and iconic bottle.

12

The "Lady Dior" bag is one of the brand's most iconic accessories, which has become synonymous with timeless elegance and refinement since its creation in 1995, as a tribute to **Princess Diana.**

PREVIEW

[BAGS]

Dior bags, synonymous with elegance and luxury, have gained worldwide fame, particularly with iconic models such as the "Lady Dior", named in honor of Princess Diana. Each Dior bag reflects exceptional craftsmanship, combining innovative design and high-quality materials, making them popular pieces in the fashion industry and among luxury enthusiasts.

TRENDS
PROJECTS
COLLECTIONS
FACES
DESIGNERS
AWARDS

PARIS ⊕
WWW.DIOR.COM

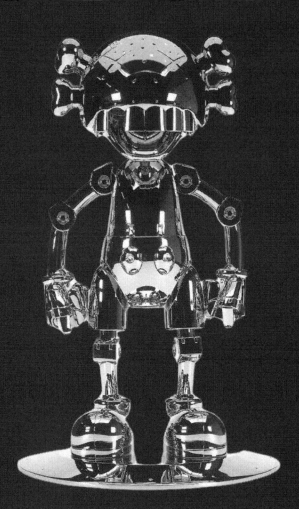

13

Dior has collaborated with various artists and designers, such as KAWS and Hajime Sorayama, integrating contemporary art and pop culture into its collections, creating unique pieces that combine fashion and art in innovative ways.

14

Against all odds, Kim Jones has joined the house of Dior as design director of Dior Homme, after leaving Louis Vuitton, leaving the fashion world to speculate about his future. This surprise appointment within the LVMH stable marked a turning point for Dior Homme, opening a new chapter under the creative vision of Jones, **while Kris van Assche took the reins of Berluti.**

15

Dior has often influenced pop culture,
appearing in films, songs and television series,
reflecting its iconic status and profound impact
on the representation of luxury and fashion in
the collective imagination.

BEN
MENDELSOHN

JULIETTE
BINOCHE

tv+

MAISIE
WILLIAMS

JOHN
MALKOVICH

CRÉER, C'EST SURVIVRE.

THE NEW LOOK

16

In this captivating series, dive into the heart of the fascinating story of **Christian Dior**, a true fashion legend, and his illustrious contemporaries such as **Coco Chanel, Pierre Balmain and Cristobal** Balenciaga, who, beyond the turmoil of World War II, were the pioneering protagonists of modern fashion, revolutionizing the world of style and elegance.

17

The brand has often integrated artistic elements into its collections.

Dior in pop culture

Dior, with its luxurious heritage and timeless aesthetic, has woven its presence into the very fabric of popular culture, transcending the boundaries of haute couture to take root deeply in the collective imagination. Through iconic film collaborations, references in popular songs or appearances in hit television series, Dior has not only maintained its relevance but also strengthened its status as the supreme symbol of luxury and elegance.

The brand's pieces, from the legendary "New Look" dress to captivating perfumes like "J'adore", are not just fashion products; they have become cultural icons, reflecting social developments and influencing trends over the decades.

This omnipresence of Dior in pop culture isn't limited to mere display; reflects a symbiotic relationship between the brand and the arts. Film, music and television creators draw inspiration from Dior's aura to enrich their works, while Dior, by embracing these media, breathes new life into his creations, making them accessible to a wider and more diverse audience.

18

By becoming a source of inspiration for artists and an object of desire for consumers, Dior demonstrates its crucial role not only as a major player in the fashion industry but also as a pillar of contemporary culture, shaping the perception of beauty, style and luxury all over the world. .

MERYL
STREEP

ANNE
HATHAWAY

LE
DIABLE
S'HABILLE EN
PRADA

19

1. **"The Devil Wears Prada"** (2006): This iconic film about the cutthroat world of New York fashion features numerous haute couture designs, including Dior pieces, worn with panache by the main characters.

20

2. **"Marie Antoinette"** (2006): For this historical film, Dior, under the direction of John Galliano at the time, created several dresses specially designed for Kirsten Dunst, who plays the role of the Queen of France.

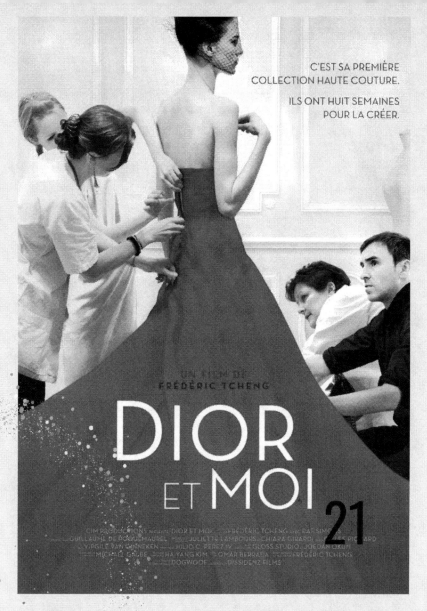

C'EST SA PREMIÈRE
COLLECTION HAUTE COUTURE.

ILS ONT HUIT SEMAINES
POUR LA CRÉER.

UN FILM DE
FRÉDÉRIC TCHENG

DIOR
ET MOI

21

CIM PRODUCTIONS present DIOR ET MOI, a FRÉDÉRIC TCHENG film with RAF SIMONS
GUILLAUME DE ROQUEMAUREL music JULIETTE LAMBOURS CHIARA GIRARDI MARK PHILLARD
VIRGILE VAN GINNEKEN JULIO C. PEREZ IV GLOSS STUDIO JORDAN OKUN
MICHAEL GALBO HAI YANG KIM OMAR BERRADA FRÉDÉRIC TCHENG
DOGWOOF DISSIDENZ FILMS

3. **"Dior et Moi"** (2014): This documentary offers
an intimate look behind the scenes of the
house of Dior, following Raf Simons' work on
his first collection as artistic director.

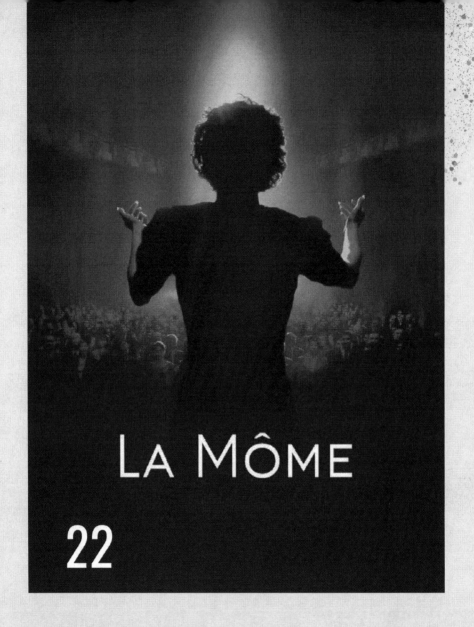

LA MÔME

22

4. **"La Môme"** (2007): Also known as "La Vie en Rose" in the United States, this Édith Piaf biopic features Marion Cotillard in costumes inspired by Dior designs, capturing the essence of the era.

23

5. **"James Bond: Casino Royale"** (2006): In this film of the James Bond saga, **Eva Green,** in the role of Vesper Lynd, can be seen wearing a stunning Dior dress in key scenes, adding a touch of glamor and sophistication .

Red carpet

One of the most memorable Dior-related stories on the red carpet involves actress **Jennifer Lawrence** at the 2013 Academy Awards That evening, Lawrence wore a sumptuous Dior Haute Couture gown when she won the Oscar for Best Actress for her role in **"Silver Linings." Playbook"**. As she climbed the steps to receive the award, she tripped due to the length of her dress. This incident, far from overshadowing her moment of glory, made her even more beloved by the public for her grace and her humor in handling this little hiccup. The dress has become iconic not only for its elegant design and contribution to an unforgettable Oscar moment, but also for highlighting the symbiotic relationship between Dior designs and defining moments in popular culture. .

24

Dior designs are a popular choice for celebrities on the red carpet.

Over the years, the Dior fashion house has dressed countless celebrities, giving them a look of timeless refinement and elegance during the most glamorous events on the red carpet. From Cannes to Hollywood, Dior creations have been the favorite choice of film, music and fashion stars, testifying to the brand's profound impact on the world of haute couture and luxury. For example, Charlize Theron, Dior's long-time muse, has often been spotted wearing the brand's spectacular dresses at prestigious ceremonies, perfectly embodying the elegance and strength that Dior wishes to convey through its creations.

Similarly, during the 2019 Oscars, actress Natalie Portman made headlines by wearing a black Dior cape embroidered with the names of unnominated directors, making her outfit a powerful political statement as well as a fashion choice.

Cannes Film Festival 2023: Natalie Portman brings Black Swan to life in a sparkling Dior dress

These iconic red carpet moments reflect the special relationship between Dior and celebrities, an alliance that goes beyond just dressing for special occasions. By choosing Dior, these personalities don't just wear a dress or suit, they embrace a rich history, exceptional craftsmanship and an artistic vision that has defined and continues to shape global fashion trends. Whether underlining a social commitment, as Natalie Portman did, or capturing the essence of modern femininity, like Charlize Theron, Dior remains an expression of power, beauty and commitment, making every red carpet appearance an unforgettable moment it's significant.

25

The Dior Café by Pierre Hermé after the battle at Solo

26

By integrating elegant cafés into some of its flagship boutiques, the Dior brand has created unique spaces where luxury and fashion meet around a refined dining experience, thus offering customers a complete immersion in the world of Dior.

THE
Christian dior
EDITION

stylist

Born on January 21, 1905 in Granville, France, Christian Dior revolutionized fashion with his "New Look" in 1947. Founder of the house of Dior, he redefined post-war feminine elegance, leaving a lasting legacy in the world of haute couture. Dior died in 1957.

Christian Dior, founder of the eponymous fashion house, revolutionized women's fashion with his "New Look" in 1947, introducing a voluptuous and elegant silhouette in stark contrast to the austere post-war styles. As a visionary and pioneer, Dior not only transformed the world of high fashion, but also left a lasting legacy that continues to influence design and aesthetics in the modern fashion industry.

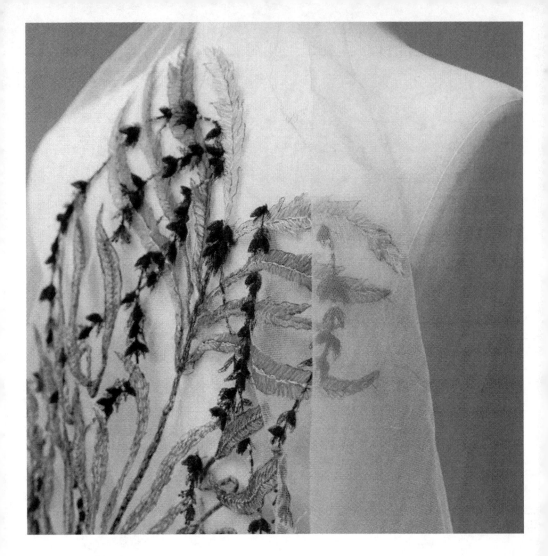

28

Dior is committed to promoting ethical and sustainable development practices in production.

29

Dior exhibitions, such as the one at the Museum of Decorative Arts in Paris, attract millions of visitors.

30

Dior continues to be a globally influential brand, synonymous with luxury, elegance and innovation, constantly setting new standards in the fashion industry through its cutting-edge design and commitment to excellence, thus captivating the imagination of customers and admirers all over the world.

31

Dior introduced the idea of
themed collections to haute
couture.

32

Metaphysical haute couture from Dior - LVMH

Dior and thematic collections: telling stories through haute couture

The House of Dior's introduction of thematic collections marked a watershed in the history of haute couture, illustrating not only the creative ingenuity of the brand but also its lasting influence on the world of fashion. These collections, designed around a specific concept or idea, allowed Dior to tell stories through his creations, thus offering an immersive and emotionally charged experience to his audience. This approach not only enriched the aesthetic dimension of the collections, but also strengthened the link between fashion and other art forms, transforming each fashion show into a captivating spectacle in which each piece contributes to an overall vision.

A famous anecdote perfectly illustrates this innovation: during the presentation of the spring-summer 2007 collection, John Galliano for Dior took inspiration from ancient Egypt, transforming the catwalk into a true celebration of the opulence and mystery of the pharaohs.

33

**Passage 01, haute couture spring-
summer 2004 | The Dior Gallery**

34

Passage 01, haute couture spring-summer 2004 | The Dior Gallery

> 66 *The models, like modern goddesses, paraded in extravagant dresses that evoked the richness of the Egyptian imagination, with sumptuous jewels and intricate embroidery. This collection remains etched in the memory as a shining example of how Dior, under the direction of visionary designers, managed to transcend the boundaries of fashion to explore new creative horizons.* 99

35

Passage 01, haute couture spring-summer 2004 | The Dior Gallery

Fashion has found beauty in other cultures for centuries.

36

The brand has often collaborated with the film industry, creating costumes for numerous films.

37

Christian Dior wrote a book called **"Je suis couturier"**, which reflects his design philosophy.

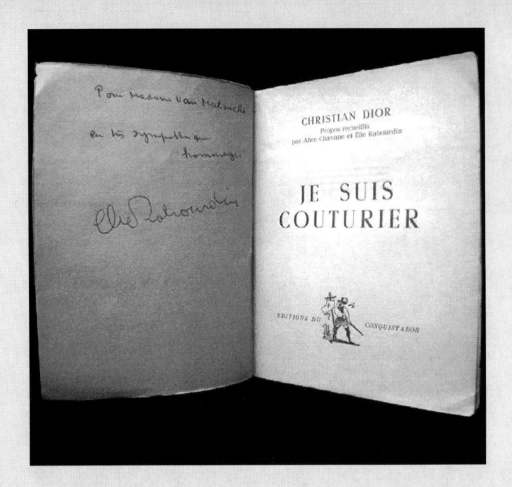

38

" *I am a couturier is the first work in which Christian Dior talks about his profession as a couturier.* "

robes étroites... »

Moi, redoutant les risques des affaires (ceux de la création me suffisant bien), je pensais rester chez Lelong toute ma vie.

Vint la Libération.

Balmain allait ouvrir, avec le succès que l'on sait, sa jeune maison.

Dès cet instant, mon travail chez Lelong me parut chaque jour plus ardu. Une grande amitié m'unissait cependant à Lucien Lelong et notre collaboration était devenue très confiante. Sans doute, la connaissance plus approfondie de mon métier, la maîtrise dont je me sentais déjà capable, me firent-elles supporter plus difficilement un tempérament si différent du mien. C'est fort possible. Je m'explique : la création d'une collection se fait en deux mois et la Mode meurt et doit mourir vite. Il est très difficile de passer une

39

"the creation of a collection is done in two months and fashion dies and must die quickly."

40

"Je suis couturier" is not only the first work in which Christian Dior confides in his profession, but it is also in this book that he reveals the fundamental principles and inspirations that guided his revolutionary vision of fashion. Through its pages, Dior shares personal anecdotes and reflections on the art of couture, offering a unique insight into the mind of one of the fashion industry's greatest innovators.

41

Before founding his fashion house, **Christian Dior designed dresses for Marshal Pétain's wife** during the Second World War, a period that profoundly influenced his desire to bring beauty and luxury back to women's lives

42

Under the leadership of Marc Bohan in the 1960s, Dior was one of the first haute couture houses to launch a **ready-to-wear line**, thus democratizing luxury and making Dior style accessible to a wider audience.

43

Dior was a **pioneer in the use of 3D to design** its collections, combining haute couture and cutting-edge technologies to create unique pieces.

44

Dior has often been mentioned in **pop music,** with references in songs by stars such as **Madonna and Rihanna**, illustrating its profound impact on popular culture.

45

The House of Dior has played a key role in the **restoration of numerous historical and cultural sites in France,** including castles and gardens, demonstrating its commitment to heritage conservation.

46

Dior perfumes are famous for their elegant bottles, especially Miss Dior's **"amphora"** design, which has become a symbol of sophistication and elegance.

Miss Dior: *an ode to love and femininity through the ages*

One of the most captivating facts about Miss Dior perfume lies in its original inspiration. When it was created in 1947, Christian Dior wanted to enclose the essence of love and femininity in a bottle, a perfumed tribute to his beloved sister, Catherine Dior, French resistance fighter and heroic figure of the Second World War. The choice of the "amphora" design for the bottle was not trivial; aimed to evoke the classic, timeless forms that symbolized female beauty and grace throughout the centuries.

This bottle, paired with Miss Dior's bold floral fragrance, immediately captured the public's imagination, becoming not only a pillar of modern perfumery but also a powerful symbol of resilience and elegance. Miss Dior is not just a perfume; it is a declaration of love, a hymn to strong and delicate femininity, which continues to inspire and seduce generations.

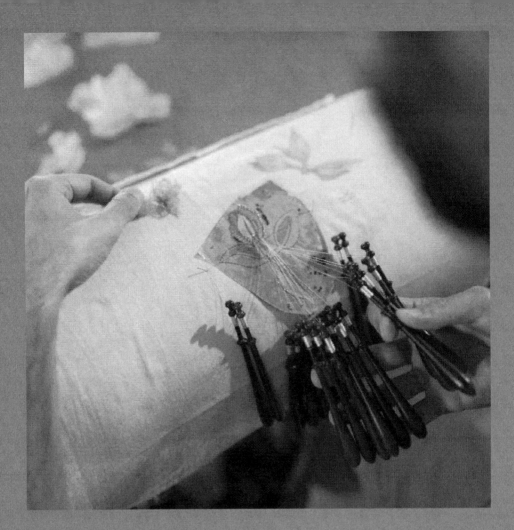

47

Dior collaborated with fine artisans
(such as embroiderers, plummers and
goldsmiths) for its haute couture collections,
underlining its commitment to excellent
craftsmanship.

DIOR STORE OF HISTORY

DIOR REINVENTS LUXURY

In the ever-changing world of fashion, the house of Dior has established itself as an innovative leader, particularly in the field of high-end shoes and sneakers.

Combining exceptional craftsmanship with cutting-edge design, Dior redefines the boundaries between traditional luxury and contemporary trends.

Dior sneakers, since their introduction, have captured the attention of the fashion world with their unique mix of sophistication and functionality.

49

Under the leadership of **Maria Grazia Chiuri,** Dior has taken strong stances in favor of gender equality, particularly through collections and advertising campaigns that carry feminist messages.

Dior with Maria Grazia Chiuri: an alliance between fashion and feminism for gender equality

Since her arrival as head of Dior's artistic direction in 2016, **Maria Grazia Chiuri has brought new energy to the brand**, marking the history of the haute couture house with her commitment to gender equality. The first woman to hold this position at Dior, Chiuri has clearly positioned the house as the voice of feminism in the fashion industry.

Through her collections, she highlighted powerful messages of empowerment and equality, integrating feminist slogans on T-shirts or drawing inspiration from strong historical female figures. For example, **its spring-summer 2017 collection was characterized by the "We Should All Be Feminists" t-shirt**, inspired by **Chimamanda Ngozi Adichie's essay**, which immediately became a symbol of this new Dior era under the sign of feminism.

Beyond the collections, Maria Grazia Chiuri ensured that these values were also reflected in the brand's campaigns and advertising initiatives.

By collaborating with female artists and supporting various causes related to gender equality, Dior, under his leadership, has actively engaged in the global debate on women's rights. This move not only strengthened Dior's identity as a socially responsible and progressive brand, but also established a dialogue with a new generation of consumers, eager to see fashion as a vehicle for positive change.

Chiuri's approach perfectly illustrates how luxury and fashion can be driving forces for female empowerment and equality, demonstrating that elegance and activism can complement each other harmoniously.

50

Under the leadership of Maria Grazia Chiuri,
Dior has transformed itself into a powerful
symbol of feminism and gender equality,
integrating messages of female empowerment
into its collections and campaigns.

51

The Christian Dior Museum in Granville regularly organizes thematic exhibitions, offering a unique insight into the history of the house and its founder and attracting visitors from all over the world interested in the history of fashion.

The Christian Dior Museum

———————————— ● ————————————

A curiosity of the Christian Dior Museum in Granville is that it is located in the villa "Les Rhumbs", Christian Dior's childhood home, beautifully perched on a cliff overlooking the sea, in the Normandy region where he spent part of his youth.

This enchanting place, with its English garden that inspired many of Dior's floral creations, was transformed into a museum in 1997 to celebrate the fiftieth anniversary of the designer's first collection.

Each year, the museum offers a new exhibition that highlights different aspects of Dior's work, from his sources of inspiration to his revolutionary contributions to fashion, allowing you to discover not only the designer's legacy but also the impact of his family and the natural environment on humans. his work.

52

In 1987, the exhibition **"Christian Dior, the other himself"** at the Richard Anacréon Museum of Modern Art in Granville initiated the creation of a fund dedicated to Dior, enriched by donations from people close to the designer, in particular his sisters Catherine and Jacqueline, as well as from acquisitions made by the city of Granville.

53

Christian Dior opened his first boutique in 1946, located at **30 avenue Montaigne in Paris,** a place that is still emblematic for the brand today, and it was in this historic space that the revolutionary "New Look" collection was presented, marking the beginning of ' a new era of fashion.

30 Avenue Montaigne: Dior's hometown

A fascinating anecdote about the first Dior boutique at 30 avenue Montaigne concerns Christian Dior's decision to choose this specific location. Even before founding his fashion house, Dior often passed by this building and dreamed of opening his own boutique in this precise place, attracted by its elegance and strategic location in the heart of Paris.

His conviction was such that he considered this place as a sign of destiny, convinced that it would play a fundamental role in his future success. This intuition proved correct, as the address became not only the birthplace of the revolutionary "New Look" collection, but also an enduring symbol of the Dior brand, embodying the very essence of Parisian luxury and elegance.

54

Christian Dior was influenced by the works of great artists such as Monet and Picasso, which is reflected in his designs.

Christian Dior: when high fashion meets Monet and Picasso

Christian Dior's inspiration, drawn from the works of masters such as Claude Monet and Pablo Picasso, profoundly influenced his approach to couture, fusing art and fashion in innovative ways. This influence manifests itself through the bold use of color, pattern and texture in his designs, borrowing from Monet a sensitivity to subtle nuance and natural beauty, and from Picasso, an appreciation for abstraction and geometry.

This artistic alchemy allowed Dior to push the boundaries of the fashion of his era, introducing silhouettes and textures that reflected not only contemporary trends but also a deep understanding of art history. By integrating these artistic influences, Dior not only consolidated his reputation as a visionary couturier, but also established a dialogue between his designs and the art world, thus enriching the visual language of haute couture.

55

Inspired by art masters such as Monet and Picasso, Christian Dior fused art and fashion in his designs, opening a new aesthetic dimension to haute couture.

DIOR EN ROSES

56

Pink was a favorite color.
Christian Dior's predilection for pink, a symbol of optimism and femininity, is expressed through the recurring use of this shade in his collections, infusing each creation with a softness and elegance that reflects his romantic and poetic vision.

57

Dior revolutionized men's suiting by introducing a more fitted and modern silhouette.

The revolution in men's suits by Dior

When the name of Christian Dior is mentioned, the image that immediately comes to mind is that of **the female revolution he started with his "New Look".** However, Dior's impact was not limited to women's wardrobe; he also made a significant contribution to men's fashion.

Dior revolutionized men's suiting by introducing a more fitted and modern silhouette, marking an important evolution in the approach to men's style. This innovation not only redefined the standards of men's elegance, but also laid the foundation for a new era in men's suit design.

An anecdote that perfectly illustrates this revolution concerns the 1957 Dior men's collection, the first to fully integrate this new vision of men's clothing. At that time, the artistic director responsible for the men's line decided to break convention by offering clothes that more closely followed the natural shape of the body.

This approach was in stark contrast to the loose cuts and boxy silhouettes that dominated the world of menswear at the time.

During an emblematic fashion show, a particularly daring dress caused a sensation: tight at the waist, with slightly defined shoulders and a cut that enhanced the silhouette without forcing it, this model was enthusiastically welcomed by an audience eager for something new.

The influence of this revolution has not faded over time. Dior clothes continue to be synonymous with elegance and innovation, inspiring generations of designers and wearers. Dior's commitment to rethinking men's clothing has not only enriched its legacy, but also established the brand as an essential reference in men's fashion.

Today, looking at contemporary collections, we can observe the living legacy of this transformation, proof that Dior's boldness and vision remain as relevant as ever.

58

Fashion Week: Dior revisits the suit for a new masculine elegance

59

Dior marked a turning point in men's fashion by introducing suits with a more **fitted and modern silhouette**, redefining masculine elegance with a cut that emphasizes shape and movement.

60

The "Junon" dress from the Autumn-Winter 1949 collection is one of Dior's most famous pieces, decorated with thousands of sequin petals.

The "Junon" dress.

The "Junon" dress from Dior's Autumn-Winter 1949 collection remains one of the most dazzling incarnations of Christian Dior's creative genius. Designed to capture the essence of the Roman goddess Juno, this wearable work of art is famous for its voluminous skirt fully embroidered with thousands of blue and green sequin petals, arranged to create an eye-catching ombré effect. Each petal has been carefully placed to mimic the beauty and fluidity of a real flower, reflecting Dior's deep admiration for nature and his talent for transforming classic inspirations into modern haute couture.

The creation of the **"Junon"** dress required hours of meticulous work and the expertise of several artisans, making it a symbol of the luxury craftsmanship and attention to detail that characterize the house of Dior. The story goes that when it first appeared, this dress not only amazed the public with its aesthetics and innovation, but also demonstrated Dior's ability to marry art and fashion in a way never seen before. The "Junon" remains a testament to Dior's legacy and cultural impact, continuing to inspire designers and fashion lovers around the world.

61

Dior launched **"Baby Dior"** in 1967, a line of luxury clothing for children which, since its introduction, has undergone a notable evolution, adapting to contemporary trends while retaining the essence of luxury and elegance that characterizes the brand, thus becoming a must. have for young fashion enthusiasts around the world.

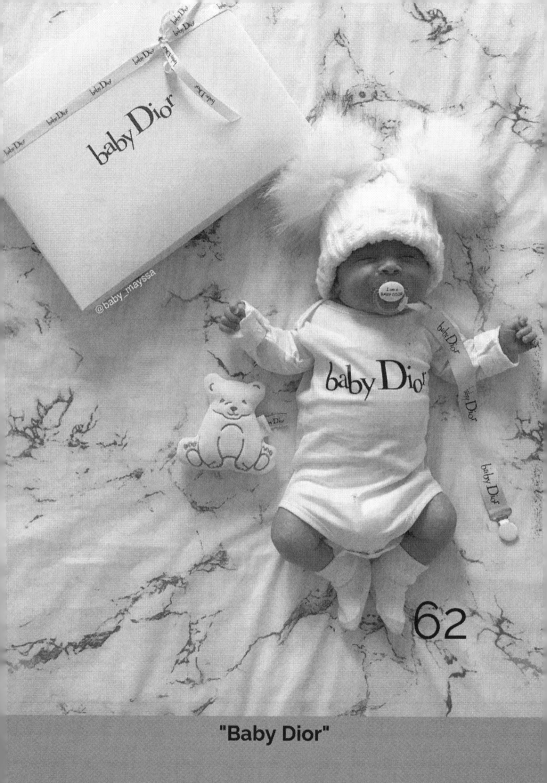

@baby_mayssa

62

"Baby Dior"

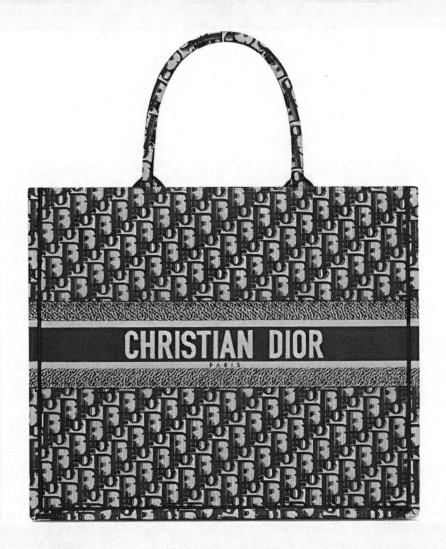

63

Introduced in 2018, the **"Dior Book Tote"** has quickly become an iconic bag for the brand.

64

In 2019, Dior designed the costumes for the **"Nuit Blanche"** ballet in Rome, marking a spectacular fusion between haute couture and dance art, where each costume reflected the elegance and artistic innovation of the house, thus strengthening the historical link between Dior and global cultural scenes.

65

Dior's **"Cruise"** shows are famous for their extravagance and location in historic locations.

66

"Sauvage" has become one of the best-selling men's perfumes in the world.

"Sauvage" by Dior: an olfactory odyssey at the pinnacle of men's perfumery

Since its launch, "Sauvage" by Dior has established itself as one of the best-selling and most recognizable men's fragrances worldwide. This fragrance, which evokes vast, wild and pristine landscapes, has captured the essence of male freedom with a bold and refined composition.

Behind its success, a perfectly balanced olfactory alchemy that combines the freshness of Calabrian bergamot, the robustness of Sichuan pepper and the depth of ambroxan, thus creating a powerful and subtle trail at the same time.

The "Sauvage" advertising campaign played a crucial role in its rise, particularly thanks to the perfume's association with charismatic muses who embody the free and wild spirit it seeks to express. Johnny Depp, with his rock star looks and undeniable charisma, has been the face of "Sauvage" since its launch.

Depp's magnetic presence in the campaigns not only strengthened the image of this fragrance, but also perfectly communicated the values of mystery, adventure and authenticity that Dior wishes to convey.

Through captivating visuals and visual narratives that evoke journeys through desert and wild landscapes, Dior and Depp have managed to create a strong identity for "Sauvage", thus distinguishing it in the competitive world of men's fragrances.

"Sauvage" is more than a perfume; it is a declaration of independence, a tribute to the indomitable spirit of modern man. Dior, relying on powerful muses and exceptional olfactory composition, not only created an iconic fragrance, but also gave new life to the concept of masculinity in perfumery.

The global success of "Sauvage" is a testament to Dior's ability to transcend fleeting trends and create timeless classics that resonate with generations of men seeking authenticity and adventure.

67

Dior organizes international exhibitions, showcasing its history and impact on fashion.

Dior in the world: exhibitions and heritage

Around the world, Dior has distinguished itself not only for its revolutionary contribution to fashion, but also for its commitment to sharing its rich heritage and cultural impact through international exhibitions.

These meticulously curated exhibitions offer visitors a journey through time, revealing the fascinating history of the house, from its founding by Christian Dior in 1946 to its current status as an undisputed symbol of elegance and innovation. Each exhibition is a celebration of the art of couture, with iconic pieces, original designs and archival materials that illuminate the creative process of its legendary designers, from Christian Dior himself to his talented successors.

These events not only highlight Dior's significant contribution to fashion, but also serve as educational platforms, inspiring new generations of designers and fashion lovers.

the importance of storytelling in fashion, showing how each collection is part of a historical and cultural continuity. From Paris to Tokyo, from Moscow to Denver, Dior's exhibitions transcend borders, affirming the house's role as a driving force in the fashion industry and a global cultural player.

Dior's international exhibitions are not simple retrospectives; they are manifestations of the house's vision, a living testimony to its perpetual influence on fashion and culture.

They close this book on Dior not as a point of arrival, but as an invitation to continue exploring and celebrating the priceless legacy of a house that, generation after generation, continues to redefine elegance, beauty and innovation.

DIOR
VALLEY FASHION
FASHION

Christian Dior's very first collection, presented in 1947, was called "La Ligne Corolle", but was nicknamed the "New Look" by the press, marking a radical change in post-war women's fashion with its voluptuous silhouettes

Dior organizes international exhibitions, showcasing its history and impact on fashion.

68

Dior's collaborations with brands such as **"RIMOWA" and "Air Jordan"** demonstrate its desire to fuse luxury with different cultures and styles, thus attracting a diverse and modern audience.

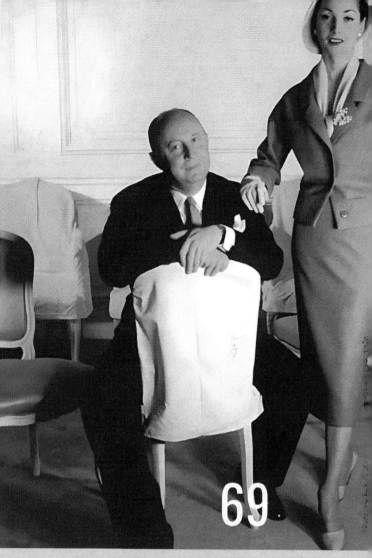

69.

After Christian Dior's unexpected death in 1957, the house was led by talented designers, each with their own vision preserving **Dior's legacy, including Yves Saint Laurent, Marc Bohan, Gianfranco Ferré, John Galliano, Raf Simons and Maria Grazia Chiuri.**

70   the art gallery

The Christian Dior Museum, located in the charming town of Granville, Normandy, is an iconic place dedicated to celebrating the legacy of the famous couturier Christian Dior. Located in Dior's childhood home, "Villa Les Rhumbs", this enchanting museum is surrounded by beautiful gardens that have been a constant source of inspiration for the designer throughout his career.

The museum offers visitors a fascinating dive into the world of Dior, displaying a rich collection that ranges from haute couture creations to photographs, through personal documents and accessories.

_____ Chloe Foster

71

Dior innovated in the world of accessories, with creations such as silk scarves and jewellery, which have become essential elements of luxury style.

66 *True elegance consists in never standing out,*

but to always be noticed. **99**

DIOR

"Luxury is freedom of thought, independence, in short kindness of the soul."

Christian Dior

Sources and References: